Whether you're a seasoned traveler, or are taking your first trip out of the country, here's every answer you'll need should a medical crisis arise on foreign soil—

- What specific inoculations you should have to protect yourself from the most common diseases to afflict Americans abroad

- How to recognize the symptoms of ordinary ailments and bring them under control by purchasing over-the-counter drugs

- How to deal effectively with time, climatic and diet changes

- Where to look for a physician overseas should you need one

And much, much more indispensable information to ensure that you retain the best possible health while visiting abroad. . . .

Medical Advice for the Traveler

BY KEVIN M. CAHILL, M.D.

POPULAR LIBRARY • NEW YORK

POPULAR LIBRARY EDITION
March, 1977

Copyright © 1970 by Kevin M. Cahill, M.D. Additional material copyright © 1977 by Kevin M. Cahill, M.D.

Library of Congress Catalog Card Number: 74-102138

Published by arrangement with Holt, Rinehart and Winston, Inc.

ISBN: 0-445-03198-0

PRINTED IN THE UNITED STATES OF AMERICA

For the Lads

Contents

Introduction   11

1. The Reasons—Why, Whether, How, When,
   Where, What   17

2. Inoculations   29
   Schedule of Immunizations   33
   Tetanus   34
   Diphtheria   34
   Polio   35
   Measles   36
   Typhoid   37
   Cholera   38
   Smallpox   40
   Yellow Fever   45
   Typhus   48
   Plague   49
   Gamma Globulin (Hepatitis)   51
   Rabies   53
   BCG (Tuberculosis)   55

3. The Medical Kit for Travelers   59

4. Advice While Traveling   83
   Time-Zone Syndrome   85
   Air Sickness   87

Food 89
Water 93
Climate 96
Clothing 98
Venereal Disease 100
Finding a Physician Overseas 101

5. The Traveler Returns 105
Medical Examination 107

Index 111

MEDICAL ADVICE
FOR THE TRAVELER

Introduction

The medical needs of the traveler are one of my major professional interests. During the past fifteen years I have attempted in practice, books and articles to present various aspects of this challenging medical problem, and yet it was almost by accident that this particular book came into being.

I accepted an invitation to discuss the medical problems of travelers before the New York Travel Writers Association and crystallized my thoughts at traffic delays between my office and the hotel where the meeting was being held some twenty blocks away. The spontaneous presentation that followed and the questions and answers of that talk were taped and published in *The New York Times*. When over 30,000 requests for the talk were received, I tried to determine why this particular presentation had appealed to so many people whereas previous attempts by myself, as well as other authors in this field, had not succeeded. I am convinced it is because today the traveler is sophisticated. Education has irrevocably altered the classic physician-patient relationship in the U.S.A., and the public will no longer docilely accept unexplained or inexplicable instructions regarding their health. The traveler, in particular, cannot afford to do so.

The tourist should want to know of the medical challenges he is to experience, but at the same time he does not wish to be deluged by irrelevant details nor frightened by elaborate clinical descriptions of preventable and controllable maladies. There certainly must be a healthy respect for the diseases of the developing lands, and yet this need not influence, adversely, the pleasures that travelers seek nor the freedom with which they explore new areas of discovery.

We have entered a new era in this world where travelers have the facility, the finances, the enthusiasm, the willingness, and even a true yearning, to see new places, and new people, and new things—and to travel in health. There are few if any areas of the world where adequate medical preparation cannot permit the most adventurous traveler to fulfill his desires.

I have attempted in the following pages to present a *common-sense* approach for preserving health while traveling. I have resisted the temptation to expand a straight-forward topic beyond its bounds, or to pad this book with extraneous lists of embassy addresses, social advice, customs data, pictures of road signs, rules regarding adequate tipping or guidelines on how best to pack a suitcase. In composing the text I approach the traveler as a fellow adventurer who is, in general, sophisticated, intelligent and interested in many facets of life, including his health. Thus I present in some detail information on indications and contraindications of inoculations and medications, not merely because these may be important facts for selected travelers to know for their own protection, but because I hope that all tourists, wanting to know more, as evidenced by their willingness to go abroad, will find the intellectual excitement and satisfaction in this fascinating field that I do. All the details presented here will *not* be necessary or relevant for every traveler—a point that will be emphasized again—but all should be of interest to the modern man. Selected for discussion are those items of particular importance to the physician protecting his patient and those questions and misconceptions that have most bothered patients who have sought my advice in recent years. Much of the attention in this book will be devoted to those medical problems that exist in the underdeveloped parts of the world. There is so little difference between living in Europe and living in the United States that to expound at length upon health problems in Western Europe would be merely reiterating advice available to the traveler from his physician at home.

As will become obvious throughout this book, I am an inveterate traveler and a great lover of the sky, and the sea, and foreign lands, and truly feel sorry for those who cannot, in our international age, take full advantage of the opportunities that are now available to so many. One writer in introducing me said, "This is Dr. Cahill; the tropics are his bag." This is only partially true, for I love many other areas and I shall try to present information for those traveling from anywhere, from Peckenham to Peshawar or New York to Nairobi.

1

The Reasons—
Why, Whether, How,
When, Where, What

In contemplating an overseas trip today the potential traveler should, at the very beginning, carefully consider *why* he is going, *whether* he should go, *how* he is to get there, *when* and *where* he is to go, and *what* he will be doing there.

The era when travel was beyond the means of most people and the reason for a trip easily defined are gone. People no longer sojourn solely for business reasons, or to complete the "grand tour," or as a post-debutante expectation, or to explore. They go for these and many other reasons today, and the latter would include merely available time, funds and means of transportation to permit a tour. Airlines entice their passengers with group tours for bachelors and for religious pilgrims, appealing to very different needs of mankind. The reason it is important, from a medical point of view, to consider why one is going is that one's expectations, reception and reactions will be greatly influenced by the motivations underlying a trip. People cannot solve their emotional problems by a geographic move, and those seeking a sun-drenched tropical paradise where work is nonexistent and women are beautiful and whiskey is cheap are almost bound to be so exceedingly disappointed that medical and psychiatric problems can be predicted. During the years that I lived in Asia and Africa, and on many overseas trips since, I have never failed to meet with nor to be amazed by the escapist. A physician sees the sad side of dreams, and I have too often been involved in efforts by either the traveler or officials of the host government to extricate the unfortunate person from the frightening disillusionment and mental disintegration that awaits the escapist.

This raises a point that Americans planning trips, especially to the developing nations of the world, should keep in mind. Anyone visiting or working in a foreign country becomes involved—willingly or unwillingly, wittingly or unwittingly—in the political intercourse of his native and host nations. Not all such contacts are felicitous. It is well for the traveler to realize that not only is he responsible for his own well-being, but that he can also contribute to or detract from the health of his homeland and seriously affect—for good or bad—the welfare of our political and diplomatic goals.

There are those who should not travel, or at least

must carefully consider whether the benefits sought are worth the dangers to be incurred. For example, the patient with severe mental disease is an extremely poor travel risk. This is so not merely while in transit, where the threat of confinement in an airplane or turbulence at sea may easily undermine a fragile mental stability, but also while in the area to which such a patient is traveling. People with inflexible, rigid attitudes may be expected to react poorly when removed from their usual environment to one where customs and principles are likely to be challenged.

This is a particular threat to those who are going to the turbulent, newly independent areas of the tropics. Somewhere in our past it became an integral part of the American heritage that we must be loved, and those with such an unrealistic and insecure feeling are not likely to do well in many parts of the world where the morning paper clearly indicates that other people simply do not feel that America is just plain wonderful.

It is very important to consider a traveler, especially one who will reside abroad, in relationship to his family. This is particularly crucial for industries with international assignments. They have an obligation to prepare and protect the traveler *and* his family. They also have a pragmatic commitment to the success of their business—be it financial or religious or anything else—and the loss of essential, trained personnel is often a burden that a budding overseas venture cannot withstand. One of the most common medical problems in our expatriate communities requiring evacuation home is mental instability on the part of families who cannot adapt either to persistent anti-Americanism or, as frequently, to the unexpected luxurious life available in many foreign lands. It is ironic that in the most poverty-stricken areas of the world the international traveler may enjoy personal service beyond his wildest expectations. As enticing as this thought may be to one laboring under our economic system, it is my experience that many are ill-suited to adapt their mores to an alien way of life or are not sufficiently secure in themselves to thrive amidst the sensual temptations of the tropics.

Another group of patients who should be cautioned about going, or certainly urged to arrange for adequate medical help before departure, are those with chronic illnesses requiring careful medical attention. The diabetic who goes in and out of coma has no business going to an area where his hosts may well not know what diabetes is and, even if they do, cannot get the drugs to manage his disease. The patient who has had multiple heart attacks should certainly go with extreme caution.

This example, however, points up one of the key dilemmas of a physician advising travelers. There are few hard and fast rules, for medicine is as much an art as a science. What a physician judges to be advisable for one particular patient may not be desirable for the next. International medical decisions, based on knowledge and experience, are humanized by their applicability to the individual traveler. They are rarely black or white decisions, but colored the most wonderful grays by factors ranging from the purely physical to those encompassing every emotion of mankind. It is my belief that one of a physician's key roles is to try, within reason, to make desires feasible. Medicine is a very personal field, and the physician has the obligation as well as the privilege to prepare the traveler for health risks and to permit him to see the balance between these and the nonmedical benefits expected from a trip.

The older-age traveler, for example, frequently poses these very challenges. A father who yearns to see a child living abroad once more before he dies cannot be realistically dissuaded from traveling except by unequivocal medical advice. There are certainly risks for this traveler, but the physician in our own urban society dealing daily with challenges greater than anything we might experience while in transit or in a developing land cannot be too dogmatic. A recent example in my office was that of an outstanding scientist who, despite several serious heart attacks, elected to go to West Africa to accomplish a work to which he had devoted the majority of his life. It would be foolhardy and wrong for a physician to categorically forbid a person from taking such a trip. I think it is our role to honestly and fairly state the challenges that are to be expected, to try to prepare the person as well as possible by pre-travel inoculations and medical management and to educate the patient to manage his own health problems to the best of his and our ability.

An obvious question that the potential traveler must consider early in the planning stage of a trip is when and where one is going. This is relevant not merely for the tropics or the Arctic, where it is painfully clear that climate will to a great degree influence one's goals and the preliminary preparations he must make. For example, the rainy season in parts of Africa precludes land travel. I well recall one research mission in which I was involved that was so ineptly planned by bureaucrats without regard for the expected floods that a group of highly paid technicians and military officers sat around a barren house for several months waiting for the sun.

It is equally important, however, for the average tourist to also incorporate climate in his plans. Many travelers seek to get out of the cold Northeastern American winters, but to go to an area where a monsoon is expected is not likely to satisfy the traveler's yearning for sun. This information should be available from one's travel agent, but can certainly be obtained from world almanacs or the local consulate or embassy of the country which one is preparing to visit. The medical indications for selecting an appropriate time to travel to an area are obvious. Heat stroke will be much more common in groups traveling to the Middle East in the summertime than in the winter, and the rainy season in Bombay is not a judicious choice for the arthritic.

The question of when one is traveling to an area will influence the type of clothing one brings, a factor that can be very important in preserving one's health in many parts of the world. The question of when one goes will also influence the type of medications that may be indicated—for example, salt tablets may be an absolutely necessary requirement if one is to travel to some areas at some seasons of the year.

How one travels is also of medical importance, and there may be strictly medical reasons why one might choose one mode of travel over another.

There are very few restrictions to air travel today. The recent lunar excursions show what aeronautical engineers are capable of, and space physicians and scientists, if necessary, can adapt an aircraft to meet almost any medical requirements. Most airlines do not permit pregnant women in their eighth or ninth month to travel, but this is as much for the sake of the airline as for the pregnant mother. There is very little indication that traveling, per se, will induce labor and there is no evidence that it will cause a miscarriage. Most airlines do not permit infants less than eight days of age to travel, but again emergency arrangements have frequently been made and completed with safety.

Although the average tourist will certainly not be faced with these problems, it is worth recording that, in general, patients with severe psychiatric disorders, especially those with manic disorders or of an unpredictable, violent nature, should not travel by air without appropriate safeguards in terms of companions, available sedatives, and restraints, if necessary. Since the range of mental disease is so broad and the numbers of psychotherapeutic drugs so vast it is impossible to give specific advice, except to emphasize that individual psychiatric assistance and careful planning are mandatory if one is required to accompany a psychiatric patient on an airflight.

There should be no restrictions for patients who have had heart disease, or who are actively suffering from angina, to travel most commercial planes. In almost all commercial airlines today oxygen is available. Many patients with cardiac disease have expressed their concern to me regarding the threat of sudden changes in cabin pressures of planes. Such pressure changes are rare, and controllable by automatically released oxygen masks, so that the cardiac patient is at no greater risk than any other passenger if such a mishap were to occur.

Those patients with middle-ear disease may experience difficulty when flying and should receive specific medical advice from their physicians before traveling. Dysbarism is an example of an ear problem that is due to inadequate equalization of pressure between the outside air and the middle ear or communicating nasal sinuses. The most common causes are an upper respiratory infection, allergy, ear or sinus inflammation. Usually the only necessary therapy for this painful syndrome is to relieve the blockage by yawning, swallowing or chewing gum. If one does have an active nasal allergy or sinusitis, then a decongestant spray (for example, Neo-synephrine) may be helpful. Antihistamines will often assist such patients in minimizing their symptoms.

2

Inoculations

The traveler can be protected against certain diseases by specific inoculations or prophylactic medications. These are the most commonly employed health procedures prior to travel, and since an awareness of the indications, contraindications, complications and efficacy are crucial to both physician and patient they will be discussed in some detail.

Most travelers deserve some inoculations and may require at least one. It is my experience, however, that there is a widespread misconception that the more one inoculates the healthier one is likely to stay; this is patently false. Inoculations and prophylactic medications should be selectively applied. To inflict unnecessary inoculations not only causes needless suffering but possible serious reactions.

All inoculations should be recorded on the yellow International Certificate of Vaccination booklet provided, in this country, by the U.S. Public Health Service. Books furnished by tourist agencies and airlines frequently do not have the necessary space for noting the manufacturer and lot number of the yellow fever vaccine, as, for example, required by international regulation. Smallpox, cholera and yellow fever vaccinations must be stamped by a certifying agency, frequently the local public health office. In major cities physicians dealing with large numbers of travelers will have a stamp available. Some travelers feel that these apparently petty details are unimportant and yet I can assure you that failure to follow them has resulted in rejection by foreign governments of very excellent inoculations. It often seems to me that there is almost an inverse ratio between the amount of attention paid to detail and the size of the country one is visiting. It behooves the wise traveler to have his immunization book in order when he arrives at the smallest airport in a foreign country.

The international certificates of vaccination, as approved by the World Health Organization, must be complete in every detail. This means that the front cover should have the name and address as requested and that on the appropriate sheets for yellow fever, smallpox and cholera the patient's name, signature, sex and age be listed. Since methods of listing dates vary in different nations it is important that the month and day be written as 11 Jan. 1960 rather than 1-11-60, which in some parts of the world would mean November 1 and may mistakenly indicate a vaccination prematurely out of date.

SCHEDULE OF IMMUNIZATIONS The traveler should contact his physician as soon as he begins planning an international trip. Ideally, the physician should have several months' time to complete a medical evaluation, education and optimal immunization program. More commonly, he is offered a few weeks as a last thought of the tourist. The resultant rush of immunizations is associated with more adverse reactions and less protective levels of immunity for certain vaccinations. The last-minute traveler will frequently receive only the required and not the recommended or optimal series of immunizations. The physician can rarely instill, in the haste of an imminent departure, a healthy respect for the medical challenges to come, nor an interest in specific diseases with instructions in their prevention.

An optimal immunization schedule for a traveler requiring multiple immunizations—*but* it must again be emphasized that no single schedule fits all travelers and inoculations should be given *only* if indicated—would take about two months. This would permit ideal spacing of inoculations to provide a maximal immunological response and minimal adverse reactions.

Knowing that necessity may preclude a long preparatory period and realizing the spontaneity with which trips are so often made today, a rush schedule of immunizations can be devised. A minimum of two weeks is required if any or all the following inoculations are indicated: typhoid, cholera, typhus, plague and rabies. Local reactions are more frequent when multiple injections are given in a short period of time. Furthermore, the protective level of immunity elicited by these inoculations is lowered as the time span between doses diminishes.

Some inoculations may be legally required—smallpox, cholera and yellow fever—for travel in certain areas, while other immunizations are only medically recommended. Such categorization is more a reflection of the concerns of history than the needs of travelers.

The following immunizations for the traveler are considered here: tetanus, diphtheria, polio, measles, typhoid, cholera, smallpox, yellow fever, typhus, plague, gamma globulin, rabies and BCG.

TETANUS–DIPHTHERIA Tetanus toxoid is a safe inoculation and by maintaining a proper level of immunity, one can avoid the danger of requiring tetanus antitoxin being administered as an emergency procedure. Tetanus is commonplace in all rural parts of the developing world. A basic series of three inoculations of toxoid is required; almost all Americans have had this in childhood. A single booster dose will stimulate adequate immunity if a tetanus inoculation had been received any time in the past ten years.

Tetanus and diphtheria are now combined in an adult preparation for single inoculation. This preparation is safe and the diphtheria toxoid has been purified so that prior skin testing (Schick testing) is no longer necessary. Reactions are minimal, and usually do not occur.

POLIO Polio is extremely rare in the United States and most Western developed countries today, but it is extremely common in the developing world. The need for polio immunization for travelers is increasing as the community level of active immunity in our own nation is decreasing. Polio vaccination is now considered an extremely safe and effective inoculation. Both the intramuscular (Salk) and the oral (Sabin) vaccines are effective. Both have been available for too short a period to determine definitely the recommended time for booster doses.

For children who have received a full series of either Salk or Sabin vaccine more than five years ago and who are to travel to endemic areas I recommend a single booster of trivalent oral (Sabin) vaccine. For adults who have received previous polio immunization, a single trivalent live oral vaccine booster is similarly recommended. If the adult has not had any previous polio vaccination, however, then two doses of the trivalent oral vaccine six to eight weeks apart are indicated. A booster dose every five years is indicated for those who reside in endemic zones.

There are theoretical contraindications to giving live virus vaccines (such as smallpox, polio and yellow fever) within several days or weeks of one another. It is often recommended that these vaccines be given at least two weeks, and preferably one month, apart. However, this is frequently unrealistic for travelers and there is a growing body of evidence that simultaneous administration of live virus vaccines is safe and effective. The U.S. Public Health Service has recently approved this procedure. It is advisable to avoid live virus vaccines being administered within two to fourteen days.

MEASLES Measles is a major disease in the developing nations of the world, and in Africa it is one of the prime causes of infant mortality. Prior to measles vaccination campaigns in the United States the skin manifestations and relatively mild systemic symptoms of the disease were well known to mothers and children throughout the land. What was not as well known was the experience that African and Asian mothers had of rapid and overwhelming pneumonia and encephalitis in their malnourished children as expected complications from measles. Whether this disease is more virulent in the tropics or the children were less able to withstand the infection is a moot point, but the traveler need not challenge himself by experimental exposure. Measles vaccine is safe and effective and is indicated for all children and adult travelers who have either not had measles or not been vaccinated previously against it.

TYPHOID Typhoid fever is a serious infectious disease affecting many organs of the body. Detailed clinical descriptions are obviously beyond our scope here but, for those interested, can be found in the textbook of tropical diseases listed among the references at the end of this book. Suffice it to note that typhoid is endemic throughout the developing world. Once common in the United States, there are now only several hundred cases reported each year in this country, and most of these result from contact with chronic carriers. Travelers to any of the endemic zones should have the benefit of typhoid vaccination, but should understand its limitations.

I suggest typhoid inoculations for visitors to every part of Africa, Southern Europe, Asia, the Philippines, the South Pacific islands, South America, Central America and rural Mexico. It is not necessary for those traveling in the Caribbean, urban Mexico, Canada, Europe, Japan, Australia or New Zealand.

The effectiveness of typhoid vaccine is less than perfect and, in the best controlled studies, a protection of only seventy to eighty per cent has been demonstrated. Paratyphoid A and B vaccines have never been proven to be effective and are now *not* advised. The father of medicine, Hippocrates, began his advice to doctors with the urging "*Primum non nocere*"—the first thing is do no harm. Paratyphoid A and B vaccines not only do no good but they significantly increase the incidence of adverse reactions.

For those who have never had typhoid inoculations before, two injections at least two weeks apart are required. For those who have had a previous typhoid series, only a single booster is necessary. An annual booster is indicated for those who will reside in an endemic area for more than a year. Injections can be given either subcutaneously (beneath the skin) or intradermally (within the skin). Most persons will experience slight redness and swelling around the injection site and some will develop fever, chills and even vomiting, headache and diarrhea, but these reactions can be minimized by taking aspirin and/or applying an ice pack locally. Because the reaction to typhoid vaccine, especially to the second inoculation, can occasionally be discomforting, I usually do not administer any other inoculation to the patient on that day. Those few travelers who have had actual clinical typhoid fever may experience marked reactions to booster inoculations. If, however, they are going to an area where typhoid is rife, and in view of the questionable duration and extent of immunity provided by an attack of typhoid, I do recommend an intradermal booster dose.

CHOLERA Cholera inoculations are required throughout Asia and in much of Africa and in some Mediterranean countries today. A major pandemic spread cholera around the world in the late sixties, and local vaccination requirements altered almost monthly. The traveler should check with his physician regarding current endemic areas. Cholera vaccination does not provide perfect protection, and one of the main values of receiving a properly valid inoculation series is to avoid having it imposed in a foreign port where sterile needles, syringes, and vaccines may well be unavailable.

Since the vaccine is not perfect, it is well for the traveler to know that cholera is transmitted by the fecal-oral route. This is a common mode of infection, and the best way a traveler can protect himself is by adhering to hygienic practices and by exercising care in avoiding contaminated water and food. Minimal contamination of water by cholera vibrios will not produce clinical cholera; one must almost drink turbid water to become infected. It is, therefore, a rare disease in tourists. In the many million cases of cholera recorded during the sixties, less than ten were in American tourists.

Two inoculations at least a week apart are necessary for those receiving the vaccine for the first time. For travelers vaccinated in the United States, a single dose is considered adequate to satisfy the international sanitary regulations, but the protection afforded by a single primary dose is not recommended. For those who will be traveling to or through endemic areas for periods of longer than six months a booster dose is required. The usual dosage for adults is a half ml. for the first inoculation and 1 ml. for the second, and appropriately smaller amounts for children. Reactions do occur and local redness and swelling at the site of injection can be minimized by aspirin and ice packs. Fever and headaches are occasionally noted.

There are no specific contraindications to cholera vaccine. Rarely a patient will experience such a severe reaction that booster dosages may be waived at the discretion of his physician, but the reason should be stated on official stationery and validated with an official stamp. Even then, it must be understood that a foreign country is under no obligation to accept an explanation when there is real danger of importing an epidemic disease of the significance of cholera.

Cholera vaccination must be recorded in the yellow book, must be properly stamped, and does not become valid until six days after a primary vaccination. Booster inoculations become valid from the day of administration. Again, it is important to date the vaccination booklet in the manner suggested previously in order to avoid confusion.

SMALLPOX Since the dawn of civilization artists have recorded the pock-marked visages of smallpox victims. Concurrent with their labors were the efforts of mankind to avoid this epidemic curse. In widely separated areas of the Middle and Far East the empiricists of antiquity discovered that scrapings from a smallpox sufferer could be placed on a chosen area of the one to be protected and a relatively minor, localized infection induced that would protect against the more extensive, often fatal, ravages of the natural disease.

Edward Jenner, an English physician, in 1796 removed material from a lesion of Sarah Nelmes, a milkmaid with cowpox, and inoculated James Phipps, a farmboy. In one of the crucial, and courageous, experiments in medical history he then exposed young Phipps to smallpox. The demonstration that inoculation with the agent of a related but mild infection will protect against a virulent disease was and is the cornerstone of modern immunization practice.

Smallpox is no longer a major disease in the world. A smallpox eradication program in West Africa in the late sixties inoculated over 100 million persons and virtually eliminated the disease in that area. Rare and small outbreaks have been recognized in recent years, however, in East Africa and Asia. The danger of epidemic smallpox spread, though more reduced than at any time in history, persists. The speed of international travel has made the tropics our neighbor. In 1962 in England, an infected man from Pakistan arrived in the town of Bradford, developed smallpox and by the time that the local epidemic had ended, twenty-seven cases had occurred, and there were four deaths. It may be of interest that nine of the cases occurred among medical personnel and three among doctors, none of whom had maintained adequate smallpox immunization.

The concept of quarantine—that a person would develop his infectious disease while on board ship or while in a holding area at the port—has been destroyed by the speed of international travel. The incubation period for smallpox is seven to twenty-one days. It is obvious that a person can fly from the endemic area of Somdia or Bangladesh to New York in eighteen hours and, for example, develop his initial lesions in Pocatello, Idaho, five or six days later where the index of suspicion will be minimal and the fact that he has recently been overseas may not even be known. In one recent outbreak of smallpox in Europe ten weeks elapsed during which twenty-three cases had occurred before the diagnosis was considered—an ample demonstration of how low the index of suspicion is in our developed world today.

Smallpox vaccination is no longer required for reentry into the United States, even when travelers are coming from an area where there has been a recent, proved outbreak of the disease. This same approach, however, is not shared by many countries, and it behooves the wise traveler to be prepared for other nations' regulations as well as his own. I recommend smallpox inoculation selectively for any travelers to Africa, Asia, or South America.

I usually employ a "multiple-pressure" method for administering smallpox vaccine. The arm should be cleansed with acetone, and *not* with alcohol, which will destroy the vaccine. The side of a sterile needle is then moved up and down ten to twenty times without breaking the skin and the vaccine permitted to soak into the skin for a moment. The remaining liquid can then be wiped off and no dressing need be applied. Other techniques have been used including the simple scratch method, but I have found fewer complications with the multiple-pressure method than with any other and I feel it should be employed. A jet injector gun permits mass vaccination, safely, of large groups.

The vaccination reaction should, if at all possible, be checked by a physician. A primary reaction, as seen in infants, occurs six to eight days after vaccination. Adults will usually experience a reaction somewhat sooner and a small pustule or vesicle or red, swollen area should be seen. If there is no reaction, a repeat vaccination is indicated since the lot of vaccine employed may not have been viable.

Smallpox inoculation is valid for international travel on the day of revaccination. For primary vaccinations it does not become valid for ten days.

Smallpox vaccination is one of the safest and most effective inoculations of man. Protection is provided for at least three years and there is evidence of a slowly falling immune level for ten years or more. Improved vaccines and vaccination techniques have reduced the number of untoward reactions to a minimum. However, as with any other procedure in medicine, there are specific contraindications—reasons why a procedure should not be employed—and specific complications that should be borne in mind.

Eczema and other chronic skin disorders are one example.

There is a distinct danger that the small, typical vaccination pustule can spread to involve all the skin areas affected by eczema. The unfortunate victim of such a "generalized vaccinia" has actually acquired smallpox rather than being protected against it. This is a particular danger for children since they cannot be expected to understand why they must not touch the itchy vaccination site and transpose smallpox virus to the rest of their body. Since children play so intimately, it is important that vaccination not be given to any member of the family in which there is an eczematous child unless specific precautions be taken to keep the affected child separated from the vaccinated person until the smallpox pustule has healed.

Pregnancy is another relative contraindication and there have been instances in every month of pregnancy where the vaccinia virus has circulated through the placenta and infected the fetus, resulting in a smallpox scarred child. There are rare occasions where a pregnant woman must go into an epidemic area and then vaccinia-immune globulin should be simultaneously administered with the smallpox vaccination.

A number of serious illnesses including leukemia, lymphoma, and dysgammaglobulinemia are other contraindications. The risk to patients on prolonged cortisone or steroid therapy must be carefully considered before vaccination is given. Once again, only in the rare instance of a full-blown epidemic, or a direct known contact with a smallpox patient, should vaccination be elected and vaccinia-immune globulin should be simultaneously administered.

Where contraindications to vaccinate occur, or if there are religious reasons prohibiting inoculations, a traveler should receive a letter on his physician's official stationery and have it certified at the Board of Health before setting out. Most countries will accept this evidence, but there is no obligation on the part of any foreign country to honor a medical note or respect an ethical belief. It is not unheard of in smaller countries of the tropics, where fear of cholera or smallpox has recently caused great emotional concern, for port authorities to insist that the patient receive a local vaccination.

Among the most common complaints from American tourists that I handled during my years in the Middle East were infected vaccinations inflicted on travelers who came unprepared to a foreign airport. If one is to travel into remote areas of the developing world requiring smallpox inoculation and cannot receive an inoculation due to a contraindication, then it is worthwhile to have the physician's explanatory letter certified by a health authority stamp.

YELLOW FEVER Yellow fever immunization is required for travelers going to any of the countries in the middle third of Africa, the northern third of South America and throughout Central America. In addition, because of local importation of a yellow fever case, a country not normally requiring yellow fever vaccination may demand it upon entry. The same, as has been noted earlier, is also true for other inoculation requirements. It is worthwhile, therefore, when traveling to those countries bordering a yellow fever endemic zone to check with your physician regarding the possibility of a recent local outbreak outdating the geographic recommendations presented here.

Yellow fever vaccine is administered at designated health centers only, primarily because the vaccine loses potency one hour after it has been reconstituted. The vaccine is a live virus vaccine and the common variety used in the United States is the 17-D strain.

Reactions to yellow fever vaccination are minimal. A very small percentage of patients may note a low-grade fever for a few days after vaccination. Only two cases of encephalitis have been reported in more than 40 million doses of vaccine administered in the United States utilizing the 17-D strain. It is not advisable that yellow fever vaccination be administered to pregnant women; a letter on the official stationery of the physician should state the reasons why vaccination is contraindicated and this explanation *may* be acceptable to a foreign government.

Other contraindications are those listed for smallpox—leukemia, lymphoma, dysgammaglobulinemia. Since yellow fever vaccination is prepared utilizing chick embryos, those who are so allergic to eggs that they are actually unable to eat them may be presumed to be allergic to the minimal egg content in yellow fever vaccine and should not be given this inoculation.

In other parts of the world the Dakar neurotropic strain is used in preparing vaccine and a significant incidence of meningoencephalitis has been reported. It is worthwhile for the traveler to obtain the recommended vaccine here before being forced to accept an alternate at a foreign airport or dockside.

The Public Health Service usually requires that smallpox and yellow fever vaccinations be separated by at least fourteen days. The problem of administering live virus vaccines (smallpox, yellow fever, measles, polio and rubella) has been alluded to before. It is my feeling that strict adherence to the fourteen-day ruling is not scientifically warranted and simultaneous administration at different sites is a feasible and safe alternative. However desirable this latter course may be it is currently not the general practice in our nation, and travelers may have to emphasize this alternative to health agencies or physicians who are yet unaware of it. In many other parts of the world simultaneous administration is being followed.

Yellow fever vaccination provides almost perfect immunity for at least ten years. At the present time, revaccination in ten years is advised, though this period may be extended in the future.

TYPHUS Typhus inoculations are not required by any country and are recommended for travelers to only a few. Typhus, a scourge in all post-war disaster areas in the history of mankind, has become extremely rare in recent years. The U.S. Typhus Commission in World War II carried out excellent vaccination and research programs and in the North African campaign not a single death occurred among those vaccinated against typhus, despite the fact that they were working in a hyperendemic area.

Typhus is endemic today only in the highlands of Ethiopia, Burundi and Ruanda in Africa, in Bolivia, Peru, Colombia, Mexico and Chile in Latin America, and in the highlands of Asia. Only travelers who will be going to rural areas in the nations listed above should receive typhus vaccine.

Two inoculations at least two weeks apart constitute a basic series. The Strain E variant of *Rickettsia prowazekii*, grown in embryonated eggs, is the typhus vaccine preferred. As noted for yellow fever vaccine, those travelers who are hypersensitive to eggs should not receive typhus vaccine since it is prepared in an egg medium.

A booster for those working in endemic areas is indicated every six months. Local redness and swelling are common reactions to typhus vaccine and can be minimized to some extent by aspirin and ice packs. The vaccine protects only against louse-borne typhus and not against murine or scrub typhus. The clinical patterns of and differences between various forms of typhus are complex, to say the least, and descriptions might be sought, by those so impelled, in the textbook of tropical medicine noted at the back of this book.

Typhus is one of those diseases for which, in my experience, protective inoculations are far too frequently provided as a routine. Any medical procedure should be selected only for those who need it. Recall the advice of sage, old Hippocrates—"*Primum non nocere.*" As many American physicians are unfamiliar with the diseases and health problems of the tropics, it is important that the patient himself be aware of the necessary inoculations, and the traveler should freely discuss with his physician the necessity for, indications and expected complications of all immunizations *before* they are administered.

PLAGUE The plague is another disease that elicits enormous emotional reaction in travelers. Most Americans are unaware that human cases of plague occur every year in the Southwestern United States among archeologists, campers and others whose duty or pleasures bring them into intimate contact with wild rodents and their infected fleas. Those with such an expected exposure might well receive plague inoculation in this country. Overseas, the only areas where plague is sufficiently endemic today to warrant general inoculation for travelers are Vietnam, Cambodia and Laos. No other traveler should receive plague vaccination unless specifically indicated by his interests and exposure. Certainly, one should not encourage all travelers to Africa, Asia or South America to be subjected to plague vaccine.

A primary vaccination series consists of three inoculations with one month between the first two, and three months between the last two. In my experience, travelers rarely provide the physician with adequate time to accomplish this series, even when it is indicated. A less desirable and partially effective course consists of two inoculations three weeks apart.

Reactions are the rule and usually consist of local reddening, swelling and warmth at the site of inoculation frequently accompanied by fever, headache, chills and vomiting.

It should again be emphasized that the geographical and occupational indications for plague vaccination are extremely restricted for travelers today, and one must be selective with inoculations if one is to avoid unnecessary discomfort or, in a small number of cases, actual harm. Plague inoculation is not required by any country today and no validated and stamped certificate, as might be required for smallpox, cholera or yellow fever, is necessary for plague vaccine. The inoculation should be recorded, however, on the back sheet of the vaccination certificate along with typhoid, tetanus and other recommended but unrequired injections.

HEPATITIS Although great attention is routinely given to smallpox, cholera, yellow fever, typhus and plague, the probability that an American tourist will acquire one of these is remote. The illness in the developing countries of the tropics that has resulted in the medical evacuations of more Americans in recent years than any other disease is one that is known here in this country—hepatitis.

Infectious hepatitis is a virus infection transmitted by the anal-oral route and, therefore, the incidence is highest where poor hygienic practices and lack of sanitary facilities are common. This is a reality in most developing countries of the world. In many of the tropical lands there is an incidence of hepatitis between five hundred to one thousand times that known in the U.S.A. Because infectious hepatitis is so common in the tropics, it is advisable that all travelers to Africa, Asia, Southern Europe, Central America, rural Mexico, South America and the Philippine and Pacific islands receive gamma globulin prior to traveling. Gamma globulin is generally not indicated for travelers to urban Mexico, the Caribbean, Canada, Europe, Australia, Japan or New Zealand. Bear in mind, however, that local outbreaks in these areas do occur, and inoculation may be advisable. For example, in 1971 Italy experienced several sanitation strikes and the incidence of hepatitis rose sharply.

Once again, this protection is not perfect but it is the best available and should be used to fullest advantage. Gamma globulin is not effective against serum hepatitis (the variety of hepatitis transmitted by transfusions, or common-needle use).

Gamma globulin is not an inexpensive vaccine. It is prepared for intramuscular injection from human blood and is therefore also not a limitless commodity. I usually give, somewhat empirically, 4 ml. of gamma globulin (or about 0.05 ml.lb.) for those traveling to endemic areas. Since the material is a bulky and gelatinous substance, I usually inject it into the buttocks where there is a bit more tissue than on the arms. There are seldom any reactions to gamma globulin inoculation other than transient, local discomfort. There is no evidence that simultaneous inoculation of gamma globulin with the other immunizations reviewed above in any way minimizes the efficacy of these vaccines.

If a person resides abroad, and if it is possible to obtain gamma globulin—as is not always the case—then a booster dose every three months is desirable. In several studies among missionaries who resided abroad for prolonged periods under village conditions, it appears that one does not acquire an immunity in proportion to duration of exposure. Attack rates of hepatitis among missionaries continued at a high level for at least the first ten years overseas.

If one does get hepatitis, then it is not uncommon for three to six months to pass before one can return to normal work. There is a definite fatality rate with clinical hepatitis. If one has not had infectious hepatitis before traveling and an acquaintance on the tour develops this disease, then without any doubt immune serum globulin administration is indicated. In fact, I frequently give gamma globulin to those who have returned without having previously received it because the incubation period for hepatitis is relatively long—somewhere between three weeks and two months.

RABIES Inoculation against rabies is occasionally indicated for *selected* travelers. Needless to say, following the bite of a rabid dog or other animal, whether in this country or abroad, there may be medical indications for administering rabies vaccine or antirabies serum, or both. Because rabies is so rampant in most of the developing nations of the world, organizations (such as the Peace Corps) whose personnel work in close proximity to animals in a rural environment give prophylactic rabies inoculations to those going to all countries except Samoa and Tonga. However, these are a unique group of travelers and I certainly do *not* recommend rabies injections for the average tourist to any nation, but only for those who might expect extensive exposure to rabid animals.

It is possible to offer rabies vaccinations today because the new duck embryo vaccine (DEV) is so remarkably safe, in marked contrast to the neurological complications that occurred with the older, nervous tissue origin rabies vaccine (Semple vaccine).

There have been very few serious reactions with the DEV strain. Only one death—whose exact relationship with the vaccine is questionable—has occurred in several hundred thousand inoculations with the rabies duck embryo vaccine. Both vaccines, however, do cause redness, swelling and pain, occasionally accompanied by fever, at the time of inoculation.

If rabies prophylaxis is elected, *after careful consideration by the physician* and the traveler who will be residing for a prolonged period in a hyperendemic area, then two 1 ml. injections of the duck embryo vaccine should be given at a one-month interval and followed six months later by a third inoculation. For the traveler with less time to prepare, three 1 ml. injections at weekly intervals will protect about eighty per cent of those inoculated against rabies. The effectiveness of the rabies vaccine should be checked a month after the final inoculation, and if no specific antibodies are noted, then further inoculations are indicated. Booster doses for those resident in a hyperendemic area are indicated every three years.

Even with the pre-exposure inoculations, however, the traveler who is bitten by a rabid dog will require careful medical management. So many factors enter the decision, following a bite by a rabid animal, as to whether or not a complete series of rabies inoculations is indicated that, if at all possible, it is very worthwhile going to a center where there is a physician experienced with rabies bites. Prophylactic rabies series *may* minimize the number of rabies injections required after a bite from fourteen painful inoculations in the abdominal wall to from only one to five injections. No hard and fast rules, can be stated, however, since the site of the bite, the type of animal, the severity of the lesions, the rapidity with which they were cleansed, will all influence the judgment of the experienced physician. Once again, medicine is as much an art as a science.

TUBERCULOSIS In most of the developing world, particularly in the tropics, tuberculosis is rife. Since this serious disease is transmitted from person to person by inhalation of infective organisms from expectorated sputum, the best protection a tourist can obtain prior to traveling through an endemic area is an awareness of the disease and a healthy respect for the mode of transmission. Common sense would indicate the advisability of avoiding close contact with known tuberculosis patients and careless coughers.

Since almost all native residents in an endemic area develop some degree of tuberculous infection, a very valuable vaccine, the BCG (or bacillus Calmette-Guérin) inoculation, is routinely advised for this population. I do *not* recommend BCG for the average American tourist to any part of the world.

Even for those who will reside in hyperendemic areas I do *not* suggest BCG. For inoculation with BCG, while useful in an endemic area, has the grave disadvantage for those from the developed areas that it alters one of the best and easiest criteria for assessing infection, the tuberculin test.

Most Americans today have a negative tuberculin skin test—an evidence of the absence of antibodies against tuberculosis. As part of a pre-travel medical examination a tuberculin test should be done and recorded. If, after return, a repeat tuberculin test indicates, by changing from negative to positive, a recent infection, then the traveler's physician will probably elect to employ antituberculous medication to prevent clinical establishment or spread of the infection. I much prefer a simple skin test and specific therapy, if and when indicated, for the American traveler who can obtain careful medical follow-up, to blindly providing an inoculation that is imperfect and also destroys a major parameter for measuring infection.

A useful suggestion, however, for the patient traveling to some of the developing countries, where there is great concern about tuberculosis, is to have a note on his physician's stationery stating that "On evidence of clinical examination, chest X ray and or tuberculin test on (date), I find no evidence that this patient has tuberculosis or any other infectious disease." Although such notes are not required by any international sanitary rule, they are often necessary, for example, to obtain visas or work permits in some of the smaller African countries. With this in mind, a letter of this type is occasionally worth taking along.

3

The Medical Kit
for Travelers

In addition to obtaining the recommended inoculations for a particular trip from one's physician, the traveler should also seek the opportunity of discussing the methods for avoiding and, if necessary, coping with expected health challenges overseas. Many tourists going to one of the developing countries for the first time may labor under misapprehensions that can seriously restrict the joys of travel. The theatrical concept of the tropics as a vast primitive area where everyone wilts in the noonday sun and life is preserved by oral infusions of gin and tonic can readily be dispelled. Adequate food and lodgings are available everywhere in the world. They may not meet the standard or the style that one has been led to believe is essential, but they will almost certainly suffice. During a pre-trip examination and interview the doctor may detect a medical problem, and it is obvious that any required therapy should be provided before departure.

THE MEDICAL KIT
ALL Travelers
ITEM*

1. Personal physician's report and telephone number
2. Red Cross first aid booklet
3. Assorted bandages, cotton, scissors, tweezers, thermometer, flat toilet paper, sunburn lotion
4. Aspirin
5. Antihistamines
     Chlortrimeton
     Benadryl
6. Pills for motion sickness
7. Paregoric and/or Lomotil
8. Antibiotics (tetracycline)
9. Sleeping pills

The Tropical Traveler

10. Analgesics
      codeine
      demerol
11. Disposable needles and syringes

* Instructions and dosages in text. Amounts required will depend on length of trip.

12. Salt tablets
13. Insect repellents
14. Mosquito net
15. Antimalarials (chloroquine)
16. Water-purification tablets
17. Soap

The traveler should obtain an up-to-date statement of his health, including all relevant laboratory data such as a recent electrocardiogram (especially for those with heart disease), a chest X-ray report, tuberculin reaction and any other information pertinent to the particular traveler's health needs. The physician's telephone number should be included with this report in case either the traveler or a foreign doctor desires emergency information and advice. The pre-travel interview should also serve to organize and prescribe for a personal medical kit.

There are some medicines that all travelers should have available to them, while other drugs are absolutely essential only for visitors to certain areas of the world.

The traveler will not have within reach the trusted personal physician who can decide whether or not medications should be taken. He may not find those medications he knows and has used before marketed in certain parts of the world. It behooves the physician to prepare the traveler, and the traveler himself to be equipped, to handle a number of expected illnesses.

Any traveler on regular medication should take with him an adequate supply to last the entire trip. If he is to be a resident abroad, then he should certainly have available to him a six months' supply, in order that he might have ample time to secure a source for a comparable compound in his new home or to arrange for a special shipment. All medications should be clearly labeled with both generic and commercial names, with exact dosages and with exact indications and advice.

Patients who wear glasses, and particularly those with contact lenses, should not only have an extra pair with them but an exact prescription of the correction required in case one has to have them made overseas.

The cardiac patient should certainly have his or her heart medicaments available, not only in the suitcase but in a handbag, lest luggage be lost. The diabetic must have his urinalysis equipment, insulin and/or oral hypoglycemic compound on hand for the expected and unexpected need. Sugar substitute sweeteners are not generally available in many parts of the world and the traveler accustomed to and desiring these should take them along. The patient on anticoagulants must not only have a carefully outlined regimen of medication provided for him but be certain that laboratory facilities for the necessary blood coagulation tests exist in the areas to be visited. Such a patient must be clearly informed of the danger signs of overdosage and know the methods and have the means to reverse the same.

To have maximum value the medical kit should be prepared by a physician with a specific traveler and itinerary in mind. Not only does the traveler then have the benefit of specific drugs but has a tie-line to his own personal physician, providing great solace to one who falls ill and is alone in a far-off land. The more knowledgeable a traveler is regarding health problems and their management the more valuable will the medical kit be. It behooves the traveler—especially one who will venture off the beaten path in distant lands—to become familiar with diseases he may meet and to read of the methods of transmission, clinical patterns and usual treatment.

Some of the common items recommended for a medical kit are listed on page 62. Most are self-explanatory but a few words of comment are indicated for others.

An *antihistamine* is very useful. Not only might it minimize symptoms of allergy, but it will reduce the effects of dysbarism in air travel, provide relief from itching secondary to insect bites or rashes related to exposure to unusual plant substances and permit the traveler some added rest. It is well to note that antihistamines may blur vision and may make driving a hazardous undertaking. I usually recommend Chlortrimeton, one tablet three times per day for minor symptoms, and Benadryl, one 50 mg.

tablet two to three times daily for more bothersome allergic reactions.

Paregoric is my choice as an antidiarrheal agent. I find it much more useful than Kaopectate or any of the other innumerable compounds available. Paregoric is an opiate, and, as such, provides an added benefit to the traveler experiencing serious diarrhea. It will dull, if not eliminate, abdominal cramps. I usually advise one and one-half tablespoons—or, as I have told travelers, the equivalent of a good swig or mouthful—followed by a teaspoonful after each bowel movement until the diarrhea ceases. This usually will not take more than four to five hours. Paregoric can be used to prevent diarrhea—for example, if one is to take a long bus ride and does not want the embarrassment of having to defecate along the roadside, and if one has been experiencing an increase in bowel habits, then a tablespoon of paregoric before setting out on a six- or eight-hour jaunt can be socially satisfying. Lomotil is a good alternative antidiarrheal agent and has the advantage of being marketed in tablet form. It does not, however, minimize cramps as effectively in my personal—as well as—professional experience.

I encourage, however, the average traveler who experiences a slight increase in bowel movements *not* to become distressed by this. This is to be expected. Changes in atmospheric pressure for the air traveler, the exposure to new diets, the almost universal tendency to overindulge in rich foods and alcohol on a plane or boat, the reaction to new virus strains in water, to disruption of man's normal twenty-four-hour cycle, the so-called circadian rhythm, to tension associated with travel or separation from the security of one's home, and many, many other relatively minor causes may all lead to an alteration in bowel habits. There is nothing in the Constitution that says one defecation per day is the ideal; three or four may be just as good, and if the traveler does not feel ill and is able to get about, then this increase in bowel movements should not cause distress.

It might be worth noting here that paregoric is a liquid, and for all liquid medications (or nonmedications), it is worthwhile placing them in plastic bottles with tape about the cap. Syrupy paregoric does not mix well with one's clothes in a suitcase, and glass bottles have a tendency, under alternating air pressures, to expand and contract, thus loosening the cap. Furthermore, breakage due to rough handling is always a possibility. With this in mind, it is worth asking the pharmacist to prepare your paregoric or other liquid medicaments in plastic bottles for passage.

As a single broad spectrum *antibiotic* I usually recommend tetracycline. Not only is tetracycline exceedingly useful for the management of intestinal infections, about which more will be said below, but, though not perfect for all, is a useful "shotgun" approach to upper-respiratory, sinus, ear, skin and bladder infections.

The aim of an antibiotic available to the traveler is to permit him to treat himself until he returns to his own physician or until he is able to reach adequate medical care. One of the greatest dangers that the traveler is exposed to in many parts of the world is inadequate medical care. There is a great tendency, in my experience, for the Western traveler who becomes ill and seeks the care of a locally trained physician in a developing country to be overtreated. Although many physicians, particularly in the capitals of countries in the tropics, have unusually fine medical training, the same may not be true in the outlying areas. Even more important, in some ways, is the fact that disposable needles and syringes, medications and other expected components of modern medical armamentarium are frequently not available to the clinician in the developing world. The result often is that a minor infection, from being overtreated, becomes a major illness, with serum hepatitis, noted earlier, one of the most common sequelae of medical care in the tropics.

I well recall one beautiful young lady who, having bruised her leg, sought medical care in a Near Eastern city. Several weeks later—and with constant medications, including antibiotics, antispasmodics, anticoagulants, antidepressants (for a growing anxiety about her physician's decisions)—she had severe diarrhea, a generalized allergic rash, multiple skin and internal hemorrhages and wasting of the leg muscles from disuse. Fortunately, by discontinuing all medications and gradually ambulating the poor girl, she fully recovered from an almost fatal collision with incompetency.

No matter how sophisticated a patient is in his own chosen field he is not equipped to decide whether medical advice is good or bad, and if the patient is ill in a foreign land, his judgment is likely to be even worse than normal. The best alternative is, if at all possible, to avoid medical care overseas. Quite clearly no advice on this point can be universal and the dilemma it poses is probably the most insoluble and least satisfying item in a program of medical advice for the international traveler. However, the better prepared—with knowledge and medication—the tourist is, the less likely is it that he will have to seek medical care overseas, and if he does, then the more equipped will he be to critically assess the advice given. How one ought best seek a physician overseas is considered later.

The diarrhea that warrants antibiotics while traveling frequently starts abruptly, and is associated with abdominal cramps, and often with fever, nausea and vomiting. It may persist for days or weeks, with anywhere from six to twenty bowel movements per day. Tetracycline in this situation is very useful. Not only can it be effective therapy for Shigella, a common bacterial cause of diarrhea, but is a partially effective drug against amebas. The drug should be taken in the following manner: four tablets right away, four tablets in twelve hours, and one tablet four times a day for the next four days. Although one should *not*—and I reemphasize this—should *not* take antibiotics for every diarrheal episode, once having decided that a particular attack is so unusual in its intensity, or has one of the signs or symptoms noted above, and consequently having elected to start on antibiotics, then one should continue a full four days of therapy. This is important to prevent the emergence of tetracycline-resistant organisms and necessitate therapy with more potent compounds. Self-prescribing is, admittedly, not ideal and is not recommended at home. It seems to me, however, that in general it is the lesser of two poor alternatives—self-therapy or seeking unnecessary medical help in a foreign land.

I do not believe in so-called intestinal prophylactics as a preventive for the diarrhea of travelers. There is no good evidence that any of them are effective, despite the extensive trust that travelers have in compounds such as Entero-vioform, and despite the excellent public relations campaigns the drug companies have had on their behalf. Not only are they generally ineffective but they may conceal infections—particularly amebic infections—until more serious latent effects of these diseases occur. For example, I have seen several cases of amebic abscess of the liver develop where the patient depended unwisely on intestinal sterilants and where the diagnosis could not be made at an early, treatable stage because these medications interfered with routine stool examination methods. Furthermore, there is evidence that some "intestinal prophylactics" may actually be harmful, causing a neurological disease in man.

The same danger exists for "prophylaxis" of African trypanosomiasis, or sleeping sickness. There have been suggestions that a single intramuscular administration of pentamidine isothionate (Lomodine) will provide protection for three to four months. This has never been conclusively proved. The drug is not available routinely in the United States and, therefore, such advice is likely to be confusing to the traveler since it will be impossible, in general, to fulfill. Much more important, however, is an understanding that such "prophylaxis" can permit early, treatable sleeping sickness infections to go unrecognized until the parasite has entered the brain or spinal canal. Treatment at that stage is dangerous and often ineffective. Once again, it would be preferable to treat an active disease or accept medication only in face of a full-blown epidemic than to ostrich-like deceive oneself by partial protection.

Sleeping pills are very useful to the traveler. Although I do not take them routinely, and certainly do not believe in prescribing them routinely for people residing here in the United States, they have a particular use for the international traveler. If one can time one's trip and spend the relatively boring seven-to-ten-hours' transoceanic flying time sleeping, then one will wake rested and be able to enjoy one's initial days in a new environment. The usual upset of one's circadian rhythm, combined with dietary indiscretions or overindulgence before and while on a plane, frequently leaves the passenger in a new city in a foreign country ill and exhausted. It is important that one return to one's normal rhythm as soon as possible and sleeping pills may be very useful for several days until one has reestablished a normal pattern. As with all other medications in a medical kit, it is important again to emphasize that these tablets should be clearly labeled and the indications and dosages clearly understood before departure.

Tranquilizers, in my mind, are rarely indicated, per se, for the traveler. Obviously, if one takes them routinely at home, then one may well have necessity for them while traveling. The pharmacology of tranquilizers is such that many do not act immediately and it is often seven to ten days before one may experience their effect.

Analgesics, or pain killers, are important compounds to have available while traveling, particularly to remote areas. One may break an ankle or twist a leg in a remote area and the pain killer may be lifesaving in that it permits transportation back to a major center where adequate medical care is available. I have seen, far too often, the unfortunate results of medical care provided under less than ideal circumstances in the bush because the patient could not bear the pain of transportation back to the local capital city where excellent medical facilities were available.

I usually prescribe both codeine and demerol for travelers and give specific information as to when to employ either compound. Codeine is a relatively mild pain killer and can be taken to allay the level of pain with a sprain or twisted ankle. Codeine does tend to be constipating. It should not be used more than once every six hours and not for more than one day before seeking medical care. Again, it is emphasized that these medicines are to be used in order to allow the patient to arrive at excellent medical facilities and not to substitute for medical diagnosis and care. Demerol is a much stronger compound and should be employed only for severe pain and only for a short period without proper medical supervision. One of the other advantages of having these compounds available is that they may be useful to the patient who is hospitalized.

It is worthwhile for the patient hospitalized in a developing country to supply his physician with whatever medication he has available. This will permit administration of drugs of known potency and preparation. For parenteral drugs I advise the traveler to have *disposable needles* and *syringes* with him. Adequate sterilization equipment and medical storage facilities are wanting in many parts of Africa, Asia and South America. Because of these facts, and because of the high incidence of all forms of hepatitis in the developing lands, I prescribe for travelers to the developing lands several disposable 2½ cc. syringes with No. 22 needles (for injections) and a few 10 cc. syringes with No. 20 needles (for drawing blood or draining abscesses). These are, in my mind, some of the most important items contained in the tropical traveler's medical kit.

Salt tablets are another useful aid for some travelers. In the warm, hot tropics one may lose large amounts of fluid and body salt through perspiration. It is impossible to provide a specific dose schedule to all travelers since the areas to be visited and the amount of perspiration loss vary so much. Combined with adequate replacement of fluids the traveler should have available salt tablets for *judicious* use under those conditions in which perspiration is exceedingly marked. As with all other medicines, there are dangers as well as benefits inherent in salt tablets.

There is good evidence that excessive ingestion of salt tablets to replace the sodium and chlorides lost in perspiration may actually hinder physiological or normal acclimatization to hot climates. The body is a wonderfully adaptable mechanism, and studies have shown that one of the early protective maneuvers of man to the tropics is the manufacture of sweat with a lowered salt content, enabling man to conserve his crucial chemicals. The value of gradual acclimatization will be emphasized later.

Insects are often a major problem in the tropics and adequate *insect repellents* and pyrethrum sprays for rapid insect destruction are available in almost all tropical countries. Because bedbugs and fleas are so common in many parts of Africa and Asia, I usually recommend that travelers spray their room before going down to dinner in the evening; if a darkened room with closed windows is sprayed before dinner, the majority of the insect population will be dead by the time one wishes to retire. At that time, the windows can be opened and one can sleep in reasonable comfort until morning. If insect repellents are used, they should be applied around the neck, ankles and wrists to prevent crawling insects from entering under the clothing. Obviously, in very warm, torrid areas, perspiration rapidly negates the effect of insect repellents and they are washed off easily. The insect repellent I usually recommend is diethyltoluamide (DET). It will usually allow at least four hours of protection, and may, under ideal circumstances, protect for twelve to fifteen hours.

A *mosquito net* is advisable for those who will stray far from the beaten path in the tropics. Not only will it protect the tired traveler from night-biting malarious mosquitoes, but it will often permit sleep which might be otherwise impossible. Most camping stores have handy little nylon nets weighing only a few ounces and taking up minimal suitcase space.

For those who will go to the tropical areas, the most important tablets in their medical kit are *antimalarials*. Although great progress has been made in some parts of the world in malaria eradication, all of Africa and much of Central America, South America and the Near and Far East remain endemic malarious areas—areas where infected mosquitoes still transmit this always debilitating, often fatal, disease to man.

By adhering to a proper antimalarial drug regimen and by employing common sense in insect control—including long-sleeved shirts, and mosquito netting at night when necessary—few, if any, travelers should get malaria today.

It is very important that travelers recall that a single insect bite can be responsible for a serious attack of malaria. I have had cases—and fatal ones—in patients whose only contact with a malaria zone was when their airplane made an unexpected refueling stop of an hour in an infective zone. It is important that one's itinerary be reviewed with his physician, and if there is any question of potential exposure, malaria prophylactics must be made available.

Chloroquine diphosphate is the anti-malarial of choice. In a dosage of 300 mg. base once weekly, chloroquine is highly effective and almost nontoxic. Very rare psychological reactions do occur. It can be given for years in this prophylactic dose with no ill effects. It is marketed in this country as Aralen. It is important to note that the manufacturers label their tablets so that 300 mg. base are contained in 500 mg. Aralen. The drug reaches an effective blood level within twelve hours so there is no reason to initiate prophylaxis, as was formerly true with other anti-malarials, two weeks before departure. It is important, however, that chloroquine be taken on the *same* day every week and not as the mood strikes the casual traveler.

After leaving a malarious area, it is crucial that chloroquine be continued at weekly intervals for one month. It is also necessary, at that time, to eradicate exoerythrocytic (those parasitic forms living outside the blood stream) malaria; the drug of choice is primaquine in a dosage of 15 mg. every day for fourteen days.

There are a number of questions that are frequently asked by travelers regarding antimalarials and most will be raised here. Chloroquine, the antimalarial of choice, is indicated for all visitors to all malarious areas. In chloroquine-resistant areas, such as Vietnam, there are a number of experimental approaches being tried, none of which have yet been proven completely successful. The most common in use now are combinations of chloroquine, pyrimethamine and a long-acting sulfur compound, but information on these changes so rapidly that it would be worth one's while, if one is forced to go to such an area, to obtain up-to-date recommendations from the government or a recognized specialist in tropical medicine.

Chloroquine can be given with safety to pregnant women in all stages of pregnancy. There have been no documented reports of fetal damage secondary to chloroquine. The risk of getting malaria is a substantially greater threat to the unborn baby.

Chloroquine should be given to infants who are

going to reside in or travel through a malarious area. An English manufacturer has a liquid chloroquine compound (Nivaquine) available for pediatric usage. If necessary, chloroquine tablets can be divided and administered as the weekly dose to a child, with 62.5 mg. for those weighing under fifteen pounds, 125 mg. for those weighing fifteen to thirty pounds, 250 mg. for those between thirty and sixty pounds, and a full 300 mg. adult dose (500 mg. Aralen) for those over sixty pounds. Once again, there have been no documented reports of any damage to a growing child secondary to chloroquine.

Chloroquine has few significant side effects in the dosage used in malaria prophylaxis and therapy. There have been reports of eye damage secondary to chloroquine, but these have been almost solely in those patients receiving large doses for arthritis and related generalized conditions, where the dosages employed are more than ten times the amount prescribed in malaria prophylaxis or therapy. If one is faithful to an antimalarial program with chloroquine, in an area where chloroquine resistance is not a problem, then one will not get malaria.

Chloroquine prophylaxis provides protection for not more than seven days. With this in mind, it is very important to again stress that one take one's prophylactic as prescribed—that is, every seventh day.

There are other antimalarials available, and a physician may occasionally elect, for specific reasons, to employ one of them rather than chloroquine. Except for areas where chloroquine-resistant malaria strains exist there are, in my opinion, few such reasons. Alternate choices include chlorguanide (Pamaquin), quinacrine hydrochloride (Atabrine), pyrimethamine (Daraprim), amodiaquine (Camoquin) and quinine. Methods of administration, side effects and limitations of therapy for each of these compounds should be checked by physician and/or patient before use.

Water-purification tablets should be part of every experienced traveler's kit. One can usually get along very well in almost any part of the world on bottled water, presuming that it has been bottled where it claims to have been bottled, and on other liquid replacements. However, it is not uncommon that boiling water will not be feasible and some type of water-purification arrangement must be available. There are small heaters and water-purification units available but, in general, the traveler having to use water-purification procedures may be in areas where electricity to run the heating unit or the time and convenience to arrange the water-purification apparatus are not feasible.

For these reasons, halazone or one of the equivalent iodine water purification tablets is recommended. It is important that the directions provided be carefully adhered to; for example, water must be held for thirty minutes after treatment before serving. There are some water-purification tablets that have an anti-iodine compound to take the bitter taste out before use. I do not particularly like the taste of water after use of these tablets and have always sought out one of the alternate means noted above but, nonetheless, carry the pills with me for emergency use.

Snakebite kits are a frequently requested item for the medical armamentarium of the traveler. The basic ingredients for prevention and management of snake bites are knowledge and common sense; these cannot be supplied in a handy little kit. Once again, it seems to me that unwise dependence on erroneous information coupled with wishful thinking is far more dangerous than an actual bite.

Snakes rarely bite unless provoked and most snakes are not poisonous. Those that bite should taste only leather—it is foolhardy to wander through known snake-infested areas with bare or inadequately covered limbs. An ounce of prevention is worth a pound of cure.

If one is bitten by a poisonous snake, then specific antivenoms are indicated. The commercially available all-purpose antivenoms are not recommended. Emergency care of the bite can be provided by intermittent application of tourniquets or ice packs to minimize circulation of the venom. Except under careful medical care I do not recommend the classic Boy Scout method of incising the wound and "sucking out" the poison—extensive wound infections almost always result from this very heroic procedure of dubious value.

The most important parts of a snakebite kit are thick boots, good trousers, a keen eye and, if actually bitten, equanimity under duress, first aid as noted above, a rapid transport to a medical center and a willingness to catch the offending beast and transport his dead body back for identification for *specific* antivenom, if indicated.

4

Advice While Traveling

Just as common sense is the keynote of preparing for international travel, so also is it the one essential ingredient to a safe and happy journey. Medicine, as noted, is a very individualized and personal field of endeavor, and it is impossible to advise optimally in a small book for different persons traveling to different areas for different lengths of time by different means at different seasons. There is, however, a sum of experience that will serve all travelers well while they are on tour. Many of the methods of protecting one's health during a trip have already been considered, especially in the section on the medical kit.

TIME-ZONE SYNDROME I have already briefly discussed the phenomenon of circadian desynchronization, or the time-zone syndrome, which so many air travelers experience as they move, in a matter of hours, from continent to continent. The experienced traveler will usually schedule his departure so that the least disruption possible in his normal schedule occurs. For example, if one is to take an eight-hour journey by jet from New York to London, where it is five hours later, and if one were to leave at 9 P.M. after a busy day at the office, and a hectic ride to the airport, and several farewell drinks with relatives, and if one, following an overindulgence of food and several more drinks, were to arrive in London at ten in the morning, local time, it is not difficult to imagine the consequences. Not only would the traveler be already exhausted, but he would arrive in the midst of the morning rush hour and, several hours after clearing customs, taxiing to the city hotel and registering, an unwanted breakfast—probably the third in the last few hours—would be awaiting him. Sleep—the death of each day's life, great nature's second course—would be impossible. This type of experience is so terribly common that it is worth mentioning in the above extreme fashion, for the recuperation from such an episode might well take three days. With the schedules of twentieth-century America that recuperation might account for twenty-five per cent of a European holiday planned for years.

On the other hand, the traveler who leaves after a pleasant evening's rest, reads several magazines and a book on the plane and with the use of a sleeping pill obtains a long afternoon nap will arrive rested in time for hotel registration and a siesta, and be perfectly fit for an evening's entertainment and rest in a longed-for city.

Throughout a trip one ought to bear in mind the need for common-sense management of time and schedules. The concept of thirty-two countries in a twenty-one-day tour is offensive to anyone who has delved deeply into the joys and challenge of travel. From a medical viewpoint—coordinated, as it so often is, with the esthetic—this type of traveling is as dangerous as it is useless and, in a way, abhorrent. The prudent tourist will break for a day of relaxation and complete rest every six or seven days "on the road." It is medically advisable to provide for flexibility in scheduling *before* departure. The unexpected day of diarrhea may make a rigid series of rapid plane changes as undesirable as it will be unrealistic. Exhaustion is a particular threat to the traveler over sixty years of age and to those with any history of heart disease.

AIR SICKNESS Air sickness or sea sickness is rare today. Most ships carrying commercial passengers have very effective stabilizers, while planes fly high over the turbulence that underlaid their earlier reputation for inducing immediate nausea. If, however, the traveler has experienced motion sickness in the past, then the use of tablets such as meclizine (Bonamine) or dimenhydrinate (Dramamine) or cyclizine (Marezine) is indicated. These, as with the other antihistamines mentioned earlier, however, may cause visual changes and make the traveler extremely tired. Again, it is worthwhile considering this before planning to take a rent-a-car from a strange airport or port.

Some of the more practical approaches to motion sickness are to plan one's arrangements properly and, again, to use *common sense*. For example, on board ship, a room near the water line in the middle of the ship will minimize the effect of ocean rolling. Staying out on the deck and breathing sea air is helpful. It almost goes without saying that one's dietary habits are crucial, and one should certainly avoid overindulging in the tempting food or drink of the ship.

The same is true, obviously, on a plane. The best position to minimize the progressive symptoms of air sickness is the reclining one. The unfortunate flier should lie back as far as possible, try to remain calm, and keep one's eyes closed. It is difficult on a plane to focus on the horizon, as the whirling dervishes do to avoid dizziness while rapidly swirling. A further practical point on an airplane—a seat on the right-hand side is preferable for those who experience air sickness. Most turns are to the left in the circling or holding patterns that have become the rule over many of our urban airports.

While on an airplane for more than several hours, it is advisable to maintain adequate circulation by loosening one's stockings, removing one's shoes and, for women, not wearing tight girdles or garters. A periodic stretching of the legs by walking in the aisle or just standing can be helpful. This advice is particularly important for the older-age traveler, the obese and for those with heart disease or varicose veins.

FOOD Having arrived overseas, the major obstacles to a healthy trip that the traveler will experience are contaminated food and water, insects and, most important, lack of good judgment.

Especially in the developing countries where sanitary facilities are the exception rather than the rule, and where disposal of human and animal feces is not effectively controlled by government agencies as it is in this country, nor restricted by social mores, the possibility that anal-oral transmitted diseases will occur is high. For example, hepatitis, a serious anal-oral transmitted disease, is five hundred to one thousand times more common in almost all developing countries than it is in our own nation. Typhoid and many intestinal parasites are exceedingly common sequelae of contamination in these areas. Some of them can be prevented by inoculations obtained before traveling, but most can best be avoided by adhering to a number of simple common-sense rules.

It is absolutely necessary that proper hygienic measures be maintained during a trip to or residence in a developing country, particularly in the tropics.

Careful handwashing after toilet is, of course, a must. The same should certainly be demanded of domestic help employed overseas by those who will reside there. It is obviously impossible to depend upon a similar level of care, cleanliness or thorough hygiene of hotel staff dealing with transient populations. The burden for avoiding fecal-oral contamination lies with the traveler, and not with the cook or waiter. Even were the servant to adhere strictly to the recommendations of his employer, it is likely that, following work, he would be so amply exposed to contamination elsewhere in his native environment that one cannot depend upon his being free of disease.

One must strictly forsake the foods and liquids that are notorious vehicles for infective organisms. Cold plates, custards, pastries or any foods that have obviously been prepared long in advance of serving, should be avoided. Flies are often mechanical vehicles for feces, and the cold platter is but one of many obvious dangers that the unwary traveler is subjected to.

On the other hand, by employing common sense based on a sound knowledge of some basic facts about transmission of disease, one can eat most of the delicacies of foreign countries. There is little comparison between the effects of avoidable diarrhea and time lost from a long-sought holiday in a foreign land and the minimal disappointment of missing a gustatory challenge.

All meats should be well cooked and hot when eaten in the developing lands. Beef tapeworms (*Taenia saginata*) are a common end result for those who insist on rare steak or beef tartar in the tropics. Undercooked pork can cause both a serious tapeworm infestation (*Taenia solium*) as well as another parasitic disease, trichinosis, in which small larval worms can lodge in muscles throughout the body. The religious restrictions of the Jewish and Moslem faiths against pork are examples of deductive reasoning by leaders who knew the results, if not the specific cause, of illnesses in their tribes.

Fresh fish is safe, providing it is well cooked. Raw or smoked fish may contain another variety of tapeworm (*Diphyllobothrium latum*), as well as several other organisms that can infect and parasitize man. Clams, if obtained from polluted waters, may serve, since they are eaten raw, as a vehicle for the virus of hepatitis and other ailments secondary to fecal contamination.

In the most underprivileged area of the world, well-cooked meat and fish are a safe and excellent dish. One fine way, for example, in the Arab world to dine is to savor shishkebab. This can be eaten in the dirtiest restaurant but, if made from freshly killed lamb and cooked on charcoal in front of you, it is not only delicious but safe. In fact, there are fewer challenges to the traveler who eats in small restaurants and observes the preparation of his meal than to the wealthy tourist dining in the protected "safety" of a large resort hotel where the food has been prepared hours before by staff whose health cannot be guaranteed.

All vegetables that are freshly cooked are safe. One must use discretion in determining whether vegetables served are hot for the initial time and not reheated from yesterday or the day before. This again emphasizes one of the common dangers in some of the major resorts in the tropics where taste may go more toward duck than to charcoaled lamb or beef. It is quite impossible for a restaurant to cook a duck specifically for the hungry diner, and reheated meat doused in an orange sauce that has been used over and over is hardly an advisable dish.

All fresh fruits with unbroken skins are safe. The skin should be washed first, and if there are any breaks in them, the fruit should be discarded. One should learn to peel fruit oneself. The large, chilled "fresh fruit" compote served on a tray overlooking an exotic river might well have been cut last night in an open, fly-infested kitchen before being mixed in a plate by an infected cook. One can become exceedingly adept at peeling tomatoes as well as bananas. There are few fruits or vegetables with peels that cannot be eaten anywhere in the world.

Soaking of vegetables in potassium permanganate or chlorine solutions is *not* protective. Furthermore, the taste of "chlorinated" salad is fit only for the health masochist—I don't advise it. If it is necessary to eat fresh, leafy vegetables, they should be washed and then dipped in boiling water. Immediate reaction to this advise is, "What a certain way to ruin lettuce," and yet I lived for years in the tropics, followed this advice and by chiling the lettuce after dipping, enjoyed crisp salads every evening. This is obviously important for those residing in the tropics; I would not think it is worthwhile for those traveling through on short tours, and for them I would advise abstaining.

WATER Water may be safe in some areas of the developing world, but it is rare that one can depend upon this. Obviously, in most parts of Northern-Western Europe, and in advanced Asian cities such as Tokyo, one can drink water from the faucet with the same impunity that one does in New York. However, for those on transient trips the use of bottled water or hot tea or hot coffee as liquid replacement is advisable. As I mentioned earlier, bottled water is good provided it was bottled where it was supposed to have been bottled. It is worth having the bottle brought to one's hotel table and undoing the seal oneself. One doesn't have to live for very long in any tropical country to see hotel staff or boys in the street refilling bottles of "Vichy" or "Evian" from the local water supply.

Water is the necessary ingredient in ice, and using bottled water but locally made ice is obviously foolhardy. Although one certainly cannot recommend the use of contaminated water, one should bear in mind, however, that all diseases are dose- and host-related and that a minimal exposure to contaminated water almost never causes, per se, disease. This is useful to know for the person who wishes to use a little water to wet his toothbrush or for the woman who is concerned about douching with the local supply. I have had patients who have become so obsessed with precautions about water or disease that they have actually filled their bathtub with bottled water. This is asinine.

To supplement the great fluid needs of the human body, which are obviously greater if one is losing water by excess perspiration in the tropics, one might turn, with preference, to beer. All over the world locally prepared beer, in my experience, is excellent. The alcohol content is not terribly high and one can obtain far more liquid replacement than by attempting the same with martinis or whiskey as a source. It is worth noting, however, that if one is perspiring a good deal, one becomes inebriated more easily on the same number of drinks that one could handle at home.

Wines do not travel well, and in the tropics I have rarely found a palatable bottle south of Cairo, north of Johannesburg, or east of Suez.

I advise travelers to avoid soft drinks in the tropics, unless one can guarantee that they have been prepared according to stateside standards, or imported. This is sometimes difficult to do and, again, one has to live overseas in the tropics for a very short period before one sees the local cola bottles being replenished from a sugar and water mixture that is simultaneously serving a large population of flies. The sugar media are excellent bacterial cultures and I have personally managed a number of local outbreaks of bacillary dysentery secondary to the use of these compounds.

Milk is dangerous in many parts of the world. Bovine tuberculosis and brucellosis are two major veterinary problems that can be transmitted to man. Pasteurization processes are not common in many of the developing nations. Even where pasteurization plants exist but where the sterility of the bottling and capping processes leaves something to be desired, transmission of infections are common. Foods prepared from milk products are equally dangerous and should be avoided.

If one must use local milk in the tropics, one should bring it to a boil before use. Since this destroys much of the protein of milk, one must carefully consider the indications and expected value. For example, with infants one might not be nourishing them properly if one were to follow this method. Powdered milk products can become quite palatable. After several years in Africa, my children would not drink regular milk and had to be reeducated to its taste on returning to the United States.

Another common mode of contamination in the tropics is the use of unclean containers and utensils. Wiping the knife and fork and dish, if necessary, with a napkin will usually suffice. It is again important to emphasize that one cannot become too compulsive about contamination and live with any ease in most parts of the world besides the Northern-Western climates. The use of wash-and-dry napkins has proved a boon to the traveler and these can tactfully and effectively be employed to clean an obviously dirty dish in a hotel.

In many parts of Africa, Asia and South America, rivers, streams and lakes serve as the media not only for water causing dysentery but for another serious disease, schistosomiasis. This parasitic illness, requiring an intermediate snail host, is a major cause of intestinal bladder and liver problems. It can be avoided by staying out of inland fresh waters in the continents mentioned. One can, assuming there are no sharks or other reasons to avoid the water, swim in the ocean or large seas, such as the Mediterranean or Aegean, without worrying, at least about schistosomiasis. Canals throughout the tropics also harbor leptospira, the cause of another serious infection. This is one additional reason why one should neither swim nor wade through these bodies of water.

CLIMATE The traveler may experience extremes of cold, heat, and humidity, but adequate preparation and common sense are, again, the essential ingredients for maintaining health under difficult or changing climatic conditions. Man can adapt to almost any environment providing he allows adequate time for acclimatization and adopts the patterns of activity and clothing that experience has demonstrated to be the best for the area visited.

In the tropics extremes of heat and humidity pose medical problems for the traveler from a temperate climate. It is well to remember, however, that New York in the summertime is hardly temperate, and just as one judiciously avoids extreme exercise and exposure on a torrid day in the United States, so also must one use common sense in dealing with the same problem anywhere from Karachi to Kowloon. Many elegantly arranged experiments with military forces stationed in the Arabian Peninsula during World War II demonstrated that men who were gradually permitted to increase their activities over a fourteen-to-twenty-one-day period in a new climatic environment suffered far fewer effects than those who attempted full duties as soon as they arrived. Many other studies have confirmed these views and it is well for the tourist in the tropics to bear them in mind.

A person traveling from a cool area to a torrid one should not attempt vigorous physical activity for prolonged periods for at least several weeks. The social customs of many tropical cities are the best evidence of the need to adapt. Workdays frequently begin at sunup and last till late morning when, as the heat builds to its peak, a siesta is called till late afternoon when business may then resume till sunset. The construction of buildings in the tropics is another example of indigenous adaptation from which the traveler can learn. Shade is crucial and the long, overhanding awnings on streets in Africa and Asia are not merely picturesque but, more importantly, designed to protect the inhabitants from heat stroke and prostration.

CLOTHING Native clothing is another reflection of the effort of mankind to minimize the adverse effects of climatic extremes. The flowing cotton garb of the bedouin in the desert permits maximum protection from the sun's rays and provides the most efficient ventilation possible. For the tropics I usually advise loose-fitting cotton or light woolen garments. Hand labor is one of the most available commodities in most of the developing parts of the world and laundry services are rapid and inexpensive. Several changes of clothes are all that are necessary for the experienced traveler. The well-advertised wash-and-wear clothing of tightly woven synthetic fibers does not permit adequate evaporation of perspiration nor the introduction of circulating air.

Needless to say, there are many other factors besides temperature and humidity that will determine the most appropriate type of clothing. For example, for one traveling in the bush sturdy shoes and knee socks may be best. In insect-infested areas long-sleeved shirts and pants are a better protection against the bites of potentially infective vectors of disease than depending on sprays or repellents.

Many myths grew up over years about the advisability of head gear for those in tropical climates. The theatrical picture of the English colonialist with his pith helmet is as outdated as it was probably useless. Yet Noël Coward's famous quote that "Mad dogs and Englishmen go out in the mid-day sun" might serve the traveler as a succinct, wise and humorous bit of advice. In many parts of the East one will see people walking down the street with umbrellas to shade themselves from the sun. This and other practical methods of providing shade are commendable. The effects of overexposure in hot climates can be multiple.

The most obvious, frequent, early evidence is a sunburn, and many a sunny sojourn has been ruined by staying too long on the beach or links on the first day of a trip. The same advice for sunburn that works at home will work in the tropics—to avoid it if possible, by gradually acquiring a tan; to minimize the effects of the sun's rays by screening and protective lotions; and to manage the burn, if necessary, by rest, time, aspirin for an associated elevated temperature, and the use of cooling creams.

Heat exhaustion is a more serious syndrome due, in great measure, to excessive perspiration without adequate replacement of fluid and salt. It is seen most frequently in the unacclimatized who indulge in excessive activity soon after arrival in a hot climate. It is well documented that patients with heart disease adapt more slowly than healthy subjects. Furthermore, medical evidence indicates that hot and humid climates put a greater burden on the cardiovascular system than hot, dry climates; this would indicate that a longer period for acclimatization and adaptation of the body is necessary in the moist, hot jungles of West Africa, or Southeast Asia, for example, than in the desert area with a similar temperature range.

The treatment of heat exhaustion is based on replacing fluid loss, by the intravenous route, when possible, by rest and by cooling the victim. Usually only these simple steps are necessary.

A different entity, heat stroke, is of a much more serious nature. Complete circulatory collapse with associated temperature elevations to 106 or 107 degrees F. are not uncommon and, unless immediate medical care is provided, there is a high death rate. It is essential to lower the body temperature by the application of cold towels over the body and placing the subject under a fan or in an air-conditioned environment. Immersion of the victim in ice water is no longer advised. Intravenous fluids are not essential.

VENEREAL DISEASE Travelers seeking companionship or stimulated by the sensual atmosphere of foreign lands may seek sexual satisfaction overseas. It is well for the traveler to know that venereal disease is extremely rife in many of the developing parts of the world. In one of the medical surveys I directed in one African country seventy-five per cent of a randomly selected "healthy" population had positive Wassermann and V.D.R.L. tests for syphilis. Under the circumstances, a person who has sexual intercourse with a casual acquaintance must be prepared to pay the price or take necessary steps to avoid infection.

It is worth this traveler's while to discuss with his physician before departure the methods of protection and the signs and symptoms of gonorrhea and syphilis. Obviously, it is even more essential that, when necessary, tests for venereal infections and, if necessary, treatment for these diseases be promptly obtained.

FINDING A PHYSICIAN OVERSEAS If one does become ill while traveling and the illness is of an intensity or a duration that self-management does not seem sufficient, then one must seek medical care. I believe that the best way to find a physician in any country of the world is to call the American Embassy (one of its prime duties is to maintain an up-to-date list of selected medical specialists), the British Embassy (which does the same), or one's American air line or shipping line. American missionary organizations have a surprising number of medically trained personnel, including doctors, in the most remote corners of the world and it is worth seeking their advice and help, if possible.

There are several organizations that have compiled lists of physicians and make these available to travelers for a fee and (in one case) for free. The best known is Intermedic who, for a fee ranging from five to nine dollars, will provide a list of physicians that meet their criteria for training and education in 174 cities throughout the world. Another organization called the International Association for Medical Assistance to Travelers (IAMAT) provides a similar service and membership cards may be obtained at no cost. Unfortunately, in many of the turbulent, developing parts of the world the lists are all too frequently out of date before they are printed. This, at least, has been my experience throughout Africa. The physician is likely to be among the elite group of any newly independent country, and political changes in the government may suddenly make the M.D. unavailable either because he has fled or because he has assumed the newer duties of Foreign Minister or President.

It is worth emphasizing again that if a patient can avoid seeking medical care abroad, particularly in the developing nations, he would do well to do so. Not only is the patient's relationship with his own personal physician important in properly assessing symptoms and therapy, but the traveler is uniquely exposed, it seems to me, to many of the serious complications of medicine, including overtreatment and possible iatrogenic infections such as serum hepatitis induced by contaminated needles or syringes.

It is obviously important, for those who will reside overseas for months or years in a city, to locate a physician. This should not be left to the point of an emergency, when selection may be difficult and limited. As any patient would do at home it is important that, after careful questioning of other respected residents of the community, a physician be chosen and that the patient become known to him. This will help the physician in interpreting findings if he is called in the middle of the night or on an emergency.

5

The Traveler Returns

After the traveler returns home he should have a thorough *medical examination* regardless of whether or not he was ill while abroad. Obviously, if the traveler is ill, then the physician's attention will first be devoted to resolving the immediate problem and alleviating the patient's symptoms. The main value of a post-tour examination, however, is to detect latent infections and treat them before they become symptomatic. There may well have been lapses in the most protective barriers set up against fecal contamination. Even the best insecticide cannot completely eliminate the risk of mosquito- or fly-borne disease.

I have personally examined more than 7000 missionaries—in but one program for travelers—and 20 per cent of "healthy" subjects in that group had one or more parasitic infections.

The medical examination must, as emphasized so

often in this book, be personalized and the physician knowing his patient may well elect to approach this particular examination in various ways. However, it is my feeling that the post-tour medical clearance, particularly for the traveler to the tropics, should include a complete physical examination, a complete blood count, a tuberculin test—and chest X-ray, if indicated—a stool examination for ova and parasites and, often other studies including liver function tests, a proctoscopy, parasitic serologic tests, blood studies for typhoid fever, typhus, brucellosis and other infectious diseases to which the traveler might have been exposed and/or of which he has possible symptoms. Some diseases have long incubation periods and it is desirable to do a follow-up stool-and-blood analysis one to two months after return. Diseases diagnosed at the asymptomatic stage are, in general, easily treatable. It is well to reemphasize that none of the diseases acquired abroad are mysterious and that all, if detected early, can be treated and the patient restored to full health.

Even if the patient has no disease, a post-tour medical examination will frequently provide reassurance, and if the patient has been traveling under the auspices of a country, business company or other organization, there is an obligation—both moral and legal—to determine the status of the person's health before he is considered discharged from his duties.

It is, unfortunately, very common for patients who have experienced one of the more exotic diseases overseas—for example, malaria or amebiasis—to attribute every future ailment to a relapse of these infections. This is dangerous, not merely because it promotes a neurosis and encourages hypochondriasis, but because falsely attributing future problems to a disease that has long been cured may well result in the disaster of missing, at an early stage, the correct diagnosis of a treatable condition. I have seen cancer of the bowel falsely and tragically attributed to a relapse of amebiasis until it was too late to even try to do anything about the lesion; the same tale could be told over and in many ways.

Traveling is a wonderful experience and one can only feel sorrow for those who do not have the opportunity of visiting or living in foreign lands. Health can be maintained providing the proper preparations are taken before, during and after a sojourn.

Have a wonderful trip.

Index

abscesses
  amebic, 70
  draining of, 73
Africa, 20, 95, 96, 98
  hepatitis in, 51, 73
  malaria in, 75
  measles in, 36
  North, 48
  physicians in, 102
  plague in, 50
  rainy season in, 24
  smallpox in, 41
  tuberculosis in, 56-57
  typhoid in, 37
  typhus in, 48
  venereal disease in, 100
  West, 22, 100

  yellow fever in, 46-48
air sickness, 87-89
air travel
  heart disease and, 26
  pregnancy and, 25
  time-zone syndrome and,
    85-87
allergy, 65-66, 68
  nasal, 26-27
  to eggs, 47, 48
amebiasis, 69-70, 71, 109
amodiaquine, 79
analgesics, 62, 72-73
angina, 26
anti-Americanism, 22
antibiotics, 62, 67-71
anticoagulants, 64, 68

113

antidepressants, 68

antihistamines, 27, 62, 65–67, 88

antimalarials, 63, 75–79

antispasmodics, 68

antivenoms, 80–81

Aralen, 76–78

Arctic, travel to, 24

arthritis, 25, 78

Asia, 20
  cholera in, 38
  hepatitis in, 51, 73
  measles in, 36
  smallpox in, 41
  Southeast, 100; *see also* Vietnam
  typhoid in, 37
  typhus in, 48
  water in, 93–96

aspirin, 62, 99

Atabrine, 79

atmospheric pressure, changes in, 26–27, 65–67

Australia
  hepatitis in, 51
  typhoid in, 37

bacillus Calmette-Guerin, *see* BCG

BCG, 34, 55, 56

bedbugs, 74

beef, undercooked, 91

beer, locally prepared, 94

Benadryl, 62, 65–66

bladder infections, 67, 96

Bolivia, 48

Bombay, rainy season in, 25

Bonamine, 87

bowel habits, changes in, 66–67

brucellosis, 95, 108

Burundi, typhus in, 48

Cambodia, plague in, 50

Camoquin, 79

Canada
  hepatitis in, 51
  reentry regulations, 42
  typhoid in, 37

cancer, diagnosis of, 109

Caribbean region
  hepatitis in, 51
  typhoid in, 37

Central America
  hepatitis in, 51
  malaria in, 75
  typhoid in, 37
  yellow fever in, 46

Chile, typhus in, 48

chlorguaride, 79

chlorine, treating vegetables with, 92–93

chloroquine, 63, 76–79

Chlortrimeton, 62, 65

cholera, inoculation for, 32, 34, 38-40, 41, 50

chronic illness, 22

circadian rhythm, 67, 71-72, 85-87

clams, eating of, 91

climate, adaptation to, 24, 96-97

clothing, 25, 97

codeine, 62, 73

Colombia, typhus in, 48

contamination, compulsiveness about, 91-96

cortisone therapy, smallpox vaccination and, 44-45

cramps, abdominal, 66-67, 69

cyclizine, 88

Daraprim, 79

decongestants, 27

demerol, 62, 73

DET (diethyltoluamide), 75

developing countries, 21, 89-96
  hepatitis in, 51, 73, 89
  hospitalization in, 73
  measles in, 36
  medical care in, 68, 102
  polio in, 35
  rabies in, 53
  typhoid in, 37

venereal disease in, 100-101
  water in, 93-96

diabetes, 22, 64

diarrhea, 66, 68-71, 87

diethyltoluamide (DET), 75

dimenhydrinate, 87

diphtheria, inoculation for, 34, 34-35

disease, infectious, 108-109
  contaminated water and, 93-94
  venereal, 100-101
  See also illness; infection

Dramamine, 87

duck embryo vaccine (DEV), 53

dysbarism, 26, 65

dysentery, 95

dysgammaglobulinemia, 44, 47

ear, diseases of the, 26, 67

eczema, smallpox vaccination and, 44

eggs, allergy to, 47-48

encephalitis
  as complication from measles, 36
  as complication from yellow fever, 46

England, smallpox in, 40-41
Entero-vioform, 70
escapism, problems of, 20
Ethiopia, typhus in, 48
Europe, 15
    hepatitis in, 51
    smallpox in, 42
    typhoid in, 37
    water in, 93
exhaustion, 88, 99-100
expatriate communities
    medical problems of, 22

Far East, 75; see also Asia
fever, 69, 98-99
fish, advice on eating, 91
fleas, 74
flies, 90-93
food, advice on, 89-93
fruit, eating of, 92-93

gamma globulin, 34, 51-53
glasses, wearers of, 64
globulin, vaccinia-immune,
    44-45

halazone, 79
heart attacks, patient sub-
    ject to, 22
heart disease, 26, 63, 87, 99
heat exhaustion, 99-100
heat stroke, 24, 96-100
hemorrhage, 68

hepatitis, 51-53, 68, 73, 89,
    102
Hippocrates, 37, 49
hospitalization, 73
hypochondriasis, 109

IAMAT, 102
ice, hazards of using, 94
illness
    anal-oral transmitted, 89
    cardiac, 22, 26, 64
    chronic, 22
    mental, 20-22, 26
immunizations, optimal
    schedule of, 33-34
infection, 67, 70, 95, 101
    detecting latent, 107-108
infant mortality, 36
infants, travel with
    airlines and, 25
    chloroquine and, 77-78
inoculation, 29-57
insect bites, 65, 98, 107
insect repellents, 63, 74-75,
    98
Intermedic, 101
International Association
    for Medical Assist-
    ance to Travelers
    (IAMAT), 102
intestinal infections, 67-68,
    96
    See also dysentery

Japan
  hepatitis in, 51
  typhoid in, 37
Jenner, Edward, 41

Kaopectate, 66

Laos, plague in, 50
leptospira, 96
leukemia
  smallpox vaccination and, 44
  yellow fever vaccination and, 47
live virus vaccines, 35, 47
liver infections, 70, 96, 108
  See also hepatitis
Lomodine, 71
Lomotil, 66
lymphoma
  smallpox vaccination and, 44
  yellow fever vaccination and, 47

malaria, 75-79
Marezine, 88
measles, immunization for, 34, 36, 47
meclizine, 87
medical care
  hazards of, 67-69, 101-103

locating physicians for, 102
medication, 24-26, 63-64
  for tropical regions, 62-63
  prophylactic, 31
  See also names of medications, e.g., antibiotics
meningoencephalitis, 47
mental illness, 20-21, 26
middle-ear disease, 26-27
Middle East, 24
  cholera in, 38
  smallpox in, 40
  vaccination in, 45
milk, hazards of, 95
miscarriage, air travel and, 25
missionaries
  and finding a physician, 101
  hepatitis among, 52
monsoon, 24
mosquito net, 63, 75
motion sickness, 62, 87-89

nausea, 69, 87
Near East, 68, 75
needles and syringes, 62, 73
  and serum hepatitis, 52, 68, 102
Nelmes, Sarah, 41

Neo-synephrine, 27
New Zealand
  hepatitis in, 51
  typhoid in, 37
Nivaquine, 78
North Africa, 48

older persons, medical
    problems of, 23, 89

Pacific islands, hepatitis in,
    51
Pakistan, smallpox in, 41
Pamaquin, 79
parasites, internal, 89-90,
    96, 108
paratyphoid, vaccines for,
    37
paregoric, 62, 66-67
Peace Corps, 53
pentamidine isothionate, 71
Peru, typhus in, 48
Philippine Islands
  hepatitis in, 51
  typhoid in, 37
Phipps, James, 41
physicians, lists of overseas,
    101-103
plague, immunization for,
    34, 49-50
pneumonia, as complication
    from measles, 36

polio, immunization for, 34,
    35-36, 47
pork, hazards of eating, 91
potassium permanganate, 92
pregnancy
  air travel and, 25
  chloroquine and, 77
  smallpox vaccination and,
    44
  yellow fever vaccination
    and, 46
proguanil, 79
prophylactics, 31
  intestinal, 71
  malarial, 77-78
psychiatric disorders, 26
pyrimethamine, 79

quarantine, international
    travel and, 41-42
quinacrine hydrochloride,
    79
quinine, 79

rabies, inoculation for, 34,
    53-55
Ruanda, typhus in, 48
rubella, vaccination for, 48

Sabin vaccine, 35
Salk vaccine, 35
salt tablets, 25, 63, 73-74
Samoa, 53

Schick testing, 35
schistosomiasis, 96
sea sickness, 88
sedatives, 26
serum hepatitis, 51, 53, 68, 102
siesta, 87, 97
sinusitis, 27, 68
skin, diseases of the, 43-44, 68
skin tests, tuberculin, 55-56
sleeping pills, 62, 71-72
smallpox
    inoculation for, 34, 40-45, 51
    and yellow fever inoculation, 47
snake bite, 80
soft drinks, dysentery and, 94
South America
    hepatitis in, 51, 73
    malaria in, 75
    plague in, 50
    smallpox in, 40
    typhoid in, 37
    yellow fever in, 46
    waterborne disease in, 96
    See also Bolivia; Chile; Colombia
steroid therapy, smallpox vaccination and, 44
sulfur compounds, 77

sun, protection against, 98-100
swimming, advice on, 97
syphilis, 101

Taenia, 91
tapeworm, 91
tetanus, immunization for, 34-35
tetracycline, 62, 67-68, 69-70
time-zone syndrome, *see* circadian rhythm
Tokyo, water in, 93
Tonga, 53
tranquilizers, 72
trichinosis, 91
tropical regions, 15, 20, 61-63
    acclimatization to, 74, 97-100
    food in, 89-93
    hepatitis in, 51
    measles in, 36
    medical care in, 102
    medication for, 63
    problems of travel in, 22-25, 98-99
    smallpox in, 45
trypanosomiasis, 71
tuberculin test, 55-57, 63
tuberculosis, 55-57
    bovine, 95

examination for, 108
typhoid
    examination for, 108
    immunization for, 34, 37-38
typhus
    examination for, 108
    immunization for, 34, 48-49

United States
    plague in, 49
    reentry regulations, 42
U.S. Public Health Service, 32, 36
U.S. Typhus Commission, 48

Vaccination, International Certificate of, 31
vaccinia, 43-44
vaccinia-immune globulin, 44

varicose veins, 89
vegetables, preparation of, 92
venereal disease, 100-101
Vietnam
    malarial prophylaxis in, 77
    plague in, 50
vomiting, 69

Wassermann test, 101
water, contamination of, 93-96
water-purification tablets, 63, 79-80
West Africa, 23
wines, tropical regions and, 94
World Health Organization, 32

yellow fever, vaccination for, 34, 35-36, 45-48, 51

ABOUT THE AUTHOR

Dr. Kevin M. Cahill's involvement in the international world of the 1970's is evidenced not merely in his numerous medical research articles and books from Africa and Asia, but by his simultaneously serving now as the Director of the Tropical Disease Center, Lenox Hill Hospital, in New York City, and as Professor and Chairman of Tropical Medicine at the Royal College of Surgeons, in Ireland.

A graduate of Cornell Medical College, he received further degrees in tropical medicine from the Royal College of Physicians and from the University of London. He has had extensive field experience in Africa, Asia, and Latin America.

During his time in the U.S. Navy he served as Head of the Department of Epidemiology and Director of Tropical Medicine at the American medical research unit in Cairo, Egypt. In addition to his present academic appointments he is also consultant on tropical diseases to the United States Public Health Service, the United Nations Health Service, and to numerous foreign governments and international corporations.

Notes

Notes

Notes

Notes

Notes

Notes

Notes